Dea[r] [illegible]

[I] [illegible] will
miss your dear friend
Kathleen but she is at
last at peace and I

know she was not
happy in the nursing
home. With Deepest
Sympathy. Love &
God Bless Sharon

Blessed Are They That Mourn

"I will lift up mine eyes . . ."

Selected by Stephanie C. Oda
Designed by Betsy Beach

The C.R. Gibson Company
Norwalk, Connecticut

I will lift up mine eyes unto the hills, from whence cometh my help.

My help cometh from the Lord, which made heaven and earth.

He will not suffer thy foot to be moved: he that keepeth thee will not slumber.

Behold, he that keepeth Israel shall neither slumber nor sleep.

The Lord is thy keeper: the Lord is thy shade upon thy right hand.

Copyright © MCMLXXX by
The C.R. Gibson Company
Norwalk, Connecticut
All rights reserved
Printed in the United States of America
Formerly published under the title
I Will Lift Up Mine Eyes
ISBN: 0-8378-2020-0

The sun shall not smite thee by day, nor the moon by night.

The Lord shall preserve thee from all evil: he shall preserve thy soul.

The Lord shall preserve thy going out and thy coming in from this time forth, and even for evermore.

✒ **Psalm 121**

*I will lift up mine eyes
unto the hills,*

THE BEAUTIFUL PROMISES OF GOD

God hath not promised skies always blue,
Flower-strewn pathways all our lives through.
God hath not promised sun without rain,
Joy without sorrow, peace without pain.
God hath not promised we shall not know
Toil and temptation, trouble and woe.
He hath not told us we shall not bear
Many a burden, many a care.
But God hath promised strength for the day,
Rest for the laborer, light for the way,
Grace for the trials, help from above,
Unfailing sympathy, undying love.

AUTHOR UNKOWN

God speaks sometimes through our circumstances and guides us, closing doors as well as opening them.

He will let you know what you must do, and what you must be. He is waiting for you to touch Him. The hand of faith is enough.

PETER MARSHALL

At the onset of fear and alarm, or when trouble and stress are at hand, I will bless Him with special thanksgiving and muse upon His power, and rely on His mercies always, and come thereby to know that in His hand lies the judgment of all living, and that all His words are truth.

from THE DEAD SEA SCRIPTURES

*from whence cometh
my help.*

MYSTERIES

But this we know: our loved and dead, if
     they should come this day —
Should come and ask us, "What is life?"—
     not one of us could say,
Life is a mystery, as deep as ever death
     can be;
Yet, oh, how dear it is to us, this life
     we live and see!

Then might they say — these vanished
     ones — and blessed is the thought,
"So death is sweet to us, beloved!
     though we may show you naught;
We may not to the quick reveal the
     mystery of death —
Ye cannot tell us, if ye would, the
     mystery of breath!"

The child who enters life comes not with
     knowledge or intent,
So those who enter death must go as
     little children sent.
Nothing is known. But I believe that
     God is overhead;
And as life is to the living, so death
     is to the dead.

MARY MAPES DODGE

My help cometh from the Lord, which made heaven and earth. ℐ ℐ

THE SOUL'S INVINCIBLE SURMISE

O world, thou choosest not the better part!
It is not wisdom to be only wise,
And on the inward vision close the eyes;
But it is wisdom to believe the heart.
Columbus found a world, and had no chart
Save one that faith deciphered in the skies;
To trust the soul's invincible surmise
Was all his science and his only art.
Our knowledge is a torch of smoky pine
That lights the pathway but one step ahead
Across a void of mystery and dread.
Bid, then, the tender light of faith to shine
By which alone to mortal heart is led
Unto the thinking of the thought divine.

GEORGE SANTAYANA

EQUALITY OF GOD

Bring us, O Lord, at our last awakening, into the house and gate of heaven, to enter into that gate and dwell in that house where there shall be no darkness nor dazzling but one equal light; no noise nor silence, but one equal music; no fears nor hopes, but one equal possession; no ends nor beginnings, but one equal eternity; in the habitations of Thy glory and dominion, world without end. Amen.

JOHN DONNE

He will not suffer
thy foot to be moved:

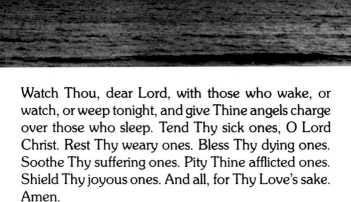

Watch Thou, dear Lord, with those who wake, or watch, or weep tonight, and give Thine angels charge over those who sleep. Tend Thy sick ones, O Lord Christ. Rest Thy weary ones. Bless Thy dying ones. Soothe Thy suffering ones. Pity Thine afflicted ones. Shield Thy joyous ones. And all, for Thy Love's sake. Amen.

ST. AUGUSTINE

I will never leave thee, nor forsake thee.

HEB. 13:5

he that keepeth thee will not slumber. 𝒟 𝒟

Cast thy burden upon the Lord, and he shall sustain thee: he shall never suffer the righteous to be moved.

PS. 55:22

There is no happiness which hope cannot promise, no difficulty which it cannot surmount, no grief which it cannot mitigate. It is the wealth of the indigent, the health of the sick, the freedom of the captive, the rest of the toiler.

CUYLER

Behold, he that keepeth
Israel shall neither
slumber nor sleep.

CONTRASTS

If all the skies were sunshine
    Our faces would be fain
To feel once more upon them
    The cooling plash of rain.
If all the world were music,
    Our hearts would often long
For one sweet strain of silence,
    To break the endless song.
If life were always merry,
    Our souls would seek relief,
And rest from weary laughter
    In the quiet arms of grief.

HENRY VAN DYKE

Come unto me, all ye that labour and are heavy laden, and I will give you rest.

MATT. 11:28

Just as there comes a warm sunbeam
into every cottage window,
so comes a love-beam
of God's care
and pity for every separate need.

NATHANIEL HAWTHORNE

Bereavement is the deepest initiation into the mysteries of human life, an initiation more searching and profound than even happy love. Love remembered and consecrated by grief belongs, more clearly than the happy intercourse of friends, to the eternal world; it has proved itself stronger than death.

Bereavement is the sharpest challenge to our trust in God; if faith can overcome this, there is no mountain which it cannot remove. And faith can overcome it. It brings the eternal world nearer to us, and makes it seem more real.

DEAN INGE

*The Lord
is thy keeper:
the Lord is thy shade
upon thy right hand.*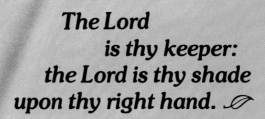

*Fear thou not;
for I am with thee:
be not dismayed;
for I am thy God.*

ISA. 41:10

THE LORD IS MY SHEPHERD

The Lord is my shepherd; I shall not want.

He maketh me to lie down in green pastures: he leadeth me beside the still waters.

He restoreth my soul: he leadeth me in the paths of righteousness for his name's sake.

Yea, though I walk through the valley of the shadow of death, I will fear no evil: for thou art with me; thy rod and thy staff they comfort me.

Thou preparest a table before me in the presence of mine enemies: thou anointest my head with oil; my cup runneth over.

Surely goodness and mercy shall follow me all the days of my life: and I will dwell in the house of the Lord for ever.

PSALM 23

Now let us thank the Eternal Power: convinced
    That Heaven but tries our virtue by
       affliction, —
That oft the cloud which wraps the present
    hour
       Serves but to brighten all our future
       days.

JOHN BROWN

The sun shall not smite thee by day, nor the moon by night.

But the nearer the dawn the darker the night,
    And by going wrong all things come right;
Things have bended that were worse,
    And the worse, the nearer they are to mend.

HENRY WADSWORTH LONGFELLOW

*If I take the wings of the morning,
and dwell in the uttermost parts of the sea;
    Even there shall thy hand lead me, and
thy right hand shall hold me.*

PS. 139: 9,10

HEAVEN OVERARCHES
EARTH AND SEA

Heaven overarches earth and sea,
    Earth-sadness and sea-bitterness.
Heaven overarches you and me:
A little while and we shall be —
Please God — where there is no more sea
    Nor barren wilderness.

Heaven overarches you and me,
    And all earth's gardens and her graves.
Look up with me, until we see
The day break and the shadows flee.
What though to-night wrecks you and me,
    If so, tomorrow saves?

CHRISTINA GEORGINA ROSSETTI

*The Lord shall preserve thee
from all evil:
he shall preserve thy soul.*

THE TIDES OF LIFE

From the beginning of time, the tides have risen and fallen and will continue to do so until the end of time. Like the tides of the sea are the tides of life. Men have been borne along, rejoicing on the crest of an incoming tide. Then it recedes, leaving much wreckage scattered along the shore.

We cannot form a true conception of life when the tide is out any more than we can obtain a true picture of the shore under the same conditions. When all things seem at low ebb, we must not give way to despondency, but must wait and work — hopefully, prayerfully, confidently — for the turn of the tide.

WALTER J. SIDNEY

GLIMPSES

I saw a star flame in the sky,
I heard a wild bird sing
And down where all the forest stirred
Another answering.

All suddenly I felt the gleam
That made my faith revive:
Ah God, it takes such simple things
To keep the soul alive.

HAROLD VINAL

*The Lord shall preserve
thy going out and
thy coming in*

HOW BEAUTIFUL TO BE WITH GOD

How beautiful to be with God,
    When earth is fading like a dream,
And from this mist-encircled shore
    We launch upon the unknown stream.

No doubt, no fear, no anxious care,
    But comforted by staff and rod,
In the faith-brightened hour of death
    How beautiful to be with God.

Then let it fade, this dream of earth,
    When I have done my lifework here,
Or long, or short, as seemeth best —
    What matters so God's will appear.

I will not fear to launch my bark,
    Upon the darkly rolling flood,
'Tis but to pierce the mist — and then
    How beautiful to be with God.

W. HALSEY SMITH

*Weeping may endure for a night,
but joy cometh in the morning.*

PS. 30:5

He giveth his beloved sleep.

PS. 127:2

from this time forth,
        and even for evermore. ✑

THERE IS A NEW MORNING

There is a new morning, and a new way,
When the heart wakes in the green
Meadow of its choice, and the feet stray
Securely on their new-found paths, unseen,
Unhindered in the certain light of day.

There is a new time, and a new word
That is the timeless dream of uncreated speech.
When the heart beats for the first time, like a bird
Battering the bright boughs of its tree; when each
To the other turns, all prayers are heard.

There is a new world, and a new man
Who walks amazed that he so long
Was blind, and dumb; he who now towards the sun
Lifts up a trustful face in skilful song,
And fears no more the darkness where his day
      began.

JAMES KIRKUP

ACKNOWLEDGMENTS

*The editor and the publisher have made every effort to trace the owner-
ship of all copyrighted material and to secure permission from copyright
holders of such material. In the event of any question arising, as to the use
of any material the publisher and editor, while expressing regret for inad-
vertent error, will be pleased to make the necessary corrections in future
printings. Thanks are due to the following authors, publishers, publica-
tions and agents for permission to use the material indicated.*

JAMES KIRKUP AND OXFORD UNIVERSITY PRESS, for "There Is A
Brand New Morning" from *A Correct Compassion And Other Poems* by
James Kirkup. Published by Oxford University Press, 1952.
LONGMAN GROUP LTD., for an excerpt from *Survival And Immortality*
by Dean Inge.
NATIONAL SELECTED MORTICIANS, for "How Beautiful To Be With
God" from *A Service Book* by W. Halsey Smith. Copyright © 1953 by
National Selected Morticians.
FLEMING H. REVELL COMPANY, for an excerpt from "The Touch Of
Faith" from *Mr. Jones, Meet The Master: Sermons And Prayers Of Peter
Marshall* edited by Catherine Marshall. Copyright © 1949, 1950 by
Fleming H. Revell Company. Renewed 1976, 1977 by Catherine Mar-
shall LeSourd.
CHARLES SCRIBNER'S SONS, for an excerpt from *The Collected
Poems Of George Santayana.* Copyright © 1923, 1951 by Charles
Scribner's Sons.

PHOTO CREDITS

Edna S. Miller—cover, pp. 3, 4, 30; James Patrick—pp. 8, 9, 16; Jeff Munk—p.
22; Gene Ruestmann—pp. 6, 7, 12; Ryan Leverkus— p. 10; Michael Powers—pp.
14, 15; Royal Carley— p. 18; Jay Johnson— pp. 20, 21; James Power—p. 24;
State of Vermont—pp. 26, 27; Cliff Fairfield—p. 29.